SLOW Journal

a guide toward groundedness

Welcome.

Take a deep breath.

I am so glad you are here. As you are. In this moment.

In your hand is a SLOW Journal, a process for grounding yourself in the present moment that you might find your way forward in harmony and wholeness in life with God.

It can be quite challenging to truly know our own experience. For many reasons – whether because the pain is too great, we believe it to be selfish, or have never been taught how to – we direct our attention and efforts elsewhere, outside of ourselves. Yet in doing so, in losing attentiveness to our own internal experiences, we often lose our bearings, even our own way.

We are most frequently lost,
not because we do not know where we are going,
but because we do not know where we are.

How we go about finding our way toward our dreams, longings, and callings has everything to do with where we find ourselves in this moment. The SLOW Journal is a guide to helping you find and ground yourself in this moment, that you might respond to the invitation of God to walk forward with God into the fullness of life.

May you find in these pages a path to greater understanding of yourself, your world, and the divine presence of God.

Brian James McMahon, LMFT

www.brianjamesconsulting.com

INTRODUCTION

The SLOW Journal is built around four reflective practices:

- [ ] **Survey** – *Where am I?*

- [ ] **Lament** – *What am I carrying? What hurts?*

- [ ] **Own** – *How is my response to my pain impacting me, my behavior, or my relationships?*

- [ ] **Welcome** – *Where is God in this?*

The power of this process does not inherently lay within the practices themselves. In many ways these practices are more like doors that we walk through into reflection, understanding, and connection. Much like the way a beautiful piece of art can transport us somewhere beyond the piece of art itself. The invitation is not to complete rigid or rote practices, but to engage in practices that invite us to places of greater depth.

As you engage, you may find your attention drawn to one practice over another from one day to the next. Remember, these practices are simply tools for your own path. Use them as is appropriate to you on any given day. Allow the Spirit to guide your attention, illuminate your internal experience, and draw you deeper into communion with God. Take what is useful, engage what is helpful, and leave the rest. I trust that the Spirit will guide you to experience the SLOW Journal in a manner that brings you more deeply into connection with God, with yourself and with others.

Three things to pay attention to as you engage this process:

- [ ] I have walked many people through this process. Often, they have found the significance to be less in what transpires in any specific day of reflection (though there may be profound individual moments for you), but in the progressive nature of the process. Much like growth in general, we often gain the greatest awareness of it after it has occurred.

☐ I have chosen to place all four practices together at the beginning of the page to provide ample space for your own reflection to influence the practice you give most attention to each day. Some days you may find yourself particularly attentive to places of lament, others to where God is present. The SLOW Journal is not intended to be a rigid script to follow, but an entry point into the places the Spirit of God might invite you.

☐ In addition to the four practices of Survey, Lament, Own, and Welcome, each day you will find yourself welcomed to the pages of reflection with a quote that I have found to be in some way related to the human experience, particularly to the human experience of challenge and pain. They are not intended to be the director of your attention and writing for the day, but simply a part of the door frame that invites you to what resides beyond it.

INSTRUCTIONS

Let us take a moment and walk through each of these practices. At the conclusion of the description of each practice I have included an example from a journal entry of my own to give you a sense of how it might work for you.

Practice 1: Survey

To **survey (S)** is to take assessment of where you are, what you are experiencing, what you are carrying, and what has happened to you. It is not to ascribe blame or to pursue solutions, but simply to ask the question, **Where am I?** and to observe what you notice.

For some, the question *Where am I?* will lead to observations of places of celebration. For others, it will bring attention to painful experiences that have been set aside in the intensity of life. It is not intended to be prescriptive (what should I now do?), but to be descriptive (what is?).

Many people I have worked with can quite readily describe where they think they "should" be, or where they dream about being, yet often have difficulty making sense of why they are not there or moving toward it.

We are most often lost,
not because we do not know where we are going,
but because we do not know where we are.

A map is only useful if you know your location on it. Where you are matters tremendously to orient yourself to where you are going. The invitation as you survey is to move slowly. **Breathe. Deeply. Again and again.** Invite the Spirit to illuminate for you where you are and what has been happening within and around you.

Here is an example of this practice, from an excerpt in my journal:

> **(S)** *I find myself thinking about something Henri Nouwen wrote about: the "strange warm pain" of "the many worlds" he was trying to keep together. Those words describe deeply the discomfort I often find myself in. That I find myself in now. The very things that seem to allow me to be the best version of myself (solitude, silence, reflection) seem to be continually at odds with the things necessary to be the best father and husband I can be. To be present with myself I withdraw. Perhaps there is a different way, perhaps I do not "have" to withdraw. But I haven't found it yet. Yet to withdraw is to offer less in those moments with my family. And it constantly feels as if those two worlds are at odds, even at war with each other. Even now as I am listening to my daughter's much-too-early morning chattering through the monitor interrupt my intended solitude, I found myself angry at my seeming inability to successfully find space for myself.*

Practice 2: (L)ament

Lament (L) is a form of mourning similar yet distinct from grief. While grief is mourning something that has been lost, lament is mourning pain and injustice that are more ongoing in nature, repeated, or perpetual. **The practice of Lament (L)** for our purposes does not exclude grief. I have chosen to draw attention to lament for the reason that much of our human struggle, pain, and suffering tend to be ongoing and repeated experiences rather than singular moments of pain and loss. Lament is mourning the presence of things that ought not to be or have been and the absence of things that ought to be or have been.

Pain is not chosen, nor does it go away when we ignore it. Disappointment, rejection, isolation, injustice. These are experiences that happen when they happen and in the way that they happen. Often, we have little control over them. Some of us try to power through. Others attempt to ignore. Sometimes we go to great lengths to provide explanations for the discomfort in life in efforts to mitigate its impact. However, ignoring it does not make it go away, powering through leads to exhaustion, and excusing it does not decrease its impact.

Lament holds room for hope that unspoken pain cannot hold.

The questions we ask in examining the lament we may hold are questions like: **Where do I hurt?** What am I holding? What am I reacting to? What is weighing on me right now?

Here is an example of this practice, continued from my journal:

> **(L)** *There is such a heaviness I feel, like a slow drift of car tires on black ice – the car slides in a direction the driver did not choose, unable to be stopped, until it finds itself landed in a snowbank. To me, this is the feeling of powerlessness to prevent inevitable failure. No matter how intentional I try to be, I do not seem to be able to regain control of my tires sliding painfully slowly across unforeseen ice on the road of my life. Whether or not I have failed, or am failing, the weight of failure's inevitability lingers within and around me. Most days this is true. Particularly today. Piercingly today. This is my lament: Once again I feel powerless.*

Practice 3: (O)wn

One of the great difficulties with the presence of pain, struggle, and suffering in our own life is the way that it impacts how we engage with ourselves, God, and others. **The practice of Owning (O) is the practice of acknowledging how the thing that we are lamenting is actually impacting how we are engaging with God, self, and/or others.** Some might call this practice "confession."

Regardless of our intent,
*It is impossible to embrace others
and protect ourselves from them at the same time;
we have to pick one.*

When we are in pain, it orients us to function from a defensive posture, which often feeds into the painful patterns in our lives. Because of this, we often become complicit in the perpetuation of our own pain or become the cause of pain to others. This does not in any way negate the injustice that happens to us, nor remove the weight of responsibility from the one who injures us. However, in order to disentangle ourselves from the impact and control of pain, we must be able to acknowledge the way that the experiences we have had have altered our behavior and the way we engage or disengage from others.

The questions we ask in examining what we might own are questions like: **how is my pain impacting my behavior and heart posture toward God, myself, or others**? What am I doing or not doing that would be different if I was not experiencing this weight or this pain?

Here is an example of this practice, continued from my journal:

> **(O)** *As I voice this lament, do you know what I hate the most? The way my felt sense of pending failure draws my heart toward bitterness and resentment. What kind of father hears his daughter reciting her ABCs to herself in the morning and finds himself resentful of her interrupting his solitude? I do. At least in this moment. I feel interrupted, inconvenienced. And I hate that I feel this way. The permeating feeling of inevitable and unavoidable failure leads me to resenting and pushing away the very people and moments which are most beautiful to me. Oh, the woundedness of my own soul.*

Practice 4: (W)elcome

At the center of the Christian narrative is the entrance of God into the suffering of God's people. God comes alongside, walks with us, talks with us, and sits with us, wherever we are. **The practice of Welcome (W) is** the invitation to be attentive to where God is, even in the midst of our lament.

Welcoming the voice and presence of Jesus loosens the grip that pain and suffering take on our identities. When we are wounded, pressed down, or disoriented, the pain often become internalized, not just to describe our experience, but they begin to define us.

As we take the time to acknowledge where we are (Survey), what hurts (Lament), and how we are responding (Own), it is imperative that we also invite the voice and presence of God to join us in that place. In doing so, we invite God to remind us of who we are and who we are becoming and to gently guide our path forward. As we draw our attention to the presence of God in the midst of our struggle, we find ourselves welcomed by God, even as we welcome God's voice.

Here is an example of this practice, continued from my journal:

(W) *Where is God in this? What would God speak to me? I find my spirit (or perhaps the Spirit of God within me) poking gently at the possibility that my feeling of failure is in some way tethered to the expectations I am placing on myself, not to what God is asking or expecting of me. I sense the possibility that the pressure I feel to "make the most" of my times of solitude is not out of longing for connection, but so that I am "settled" and "prepared" to be most "efficient" with all the tasks that await me today. It isn't to negate the value of the solitude I long for. But even here I feel Jesus reminding me that these moments of reflection and stillness are about relationship, not efficiency. When I hold solitude as useful for productivity, my daughter's interruptions set me back. When solitude is an expression of relationship, it is something I can invite my daughter into. Perhaps the obstacles I feel I am facing in finding solitude are God's way of hinting that I have once again turned relationship toward productivity. Perhaps the obstacles I am facing in finding solitude may actually be an invitation back toward connection.*

As you lean into the present moment, may you find your way forward in harmony and wholeness in life with God.

"Our efforts to disconnect ourselves from our own suffering end up disconnecting our suffering from God's suffering for us.
The way out of our loss and hurt is in and through."
Henri Nouwen

Date _____

☐ **Survey**. *Where am I?*

☐ **Lament**. *What hurts? What am I carrying?*

☐ **Own**. *How is my response to my pain impacting me, my behavior, or my relationships?*

☐ **Welcome**. *Where is God in this? What is God saying?*

_____

_____

_____

_____

_____

_____

_____

_____

_____

_____

_____

_____

_____

"Because we do not rest we lose our way... Poisoned by the hypnotic belief that good things come only through unceasing determination and tireless effort, we can never truly rest."
Ruth Haley Barton

Date _____

☐ **Survey**. *Where am I?*

☐ **Lament**. *What hurts? What am I carrying?*

☐ **Own**. *How is my response to my pain impacting me, my behavior, or my relationships?*

☐ **Welcome**. *Where is God in this? What is God saying?*

_____

_____

_____

_____

_____

_____

_____

_____

_____

_____

_____

_____

_____

_____

"If there is a meaning in life at all, then there must be meaning in suffering. Suffering is an ineradicable part of life, even as fate and death. Without suffering and death, human life cannot complete."
Victor E. Frankl

Date _____

☐ **Survey**. *Where am I?*

☐ **Lament**. *What hurts? What am I carrying?*

☐ **Own**. *How is my response to my pain impacting me, my behavior, or my relationships?*

☐ **Welcome**. *Where is God in this? What is God saying?*

_____

_____

_____

_____

_____

_____

_____

_____

_____

_____

_____

_____

_____

"Pride makes us artificial and humility makes us real."
Thomas Merton

Date _____

☐ **Survey**. *Where am I?*

☐ **Lament**. *What hurts? What am I carrying?*

☐ **Own**. *How is my response to my pain impacting me, my behavior, or my relationships?*

☐ **Welcome**. *Where is God in this? What is God saying?*

_____

_____

_____

_____

_____

_____

_____

_____

_____

_____

_____

_____

_____

*"God is a God of the present.
God is always in the moment, be that moment hard
or easy, joyful or painful"*
Henri Nouwen

Date _____

☐ **Survey**. *Where am I?*

☐ **Lament**. *What hurts? What am I carrying?*

☐ **Own**. *How is my response to my pain impacting me, my behavior, or my relationships?*

☐ **Welcome**. *Where is God in this? What is God saying?*

_____

_____

_____

_____

_____

_____

_____

_____

_____

_____

_____

_____

_____

"One can never wrestle enough with God if one does so out of a pure regard for truth."
Simone Weil

Date _____

- ☐ **Survey**. *Where am I?*

- ☐ **Lament**. *What hurts? What am I carrying?*

- ☐ **Own**. *How is my response to my pain impacting me, my behavior, or my relationships?*

- ☐ **Welcome**. *Where is God in this? What is God saying?*

_____

_____

_____

_____

_____

_____

_____

_____

_____

_____

_____

_____

_____

"There is no such thing as perfect security, only varying levels of insecurity."
Salman Rushdie

Date _____

☐ **Survey**. *Where am I?*

☐ **Lament**. *What hurts? What am I carrying?*

☐ **Own**. *How is my response to my pain impacting me, my behavior, or my relationships?*

☐ **Welcome**. *Where is God in this? What is God saying?*

_____

_____

_____

_____

_____

_____

_____

_____

_____

_____

_____

_____

_____

*"Lament opens space for hope that
unspoken pain cannot hold."*
BrianJames McMahon

Date _____

☐ **Survey**. *Where am I?*

☐ **Lament**. *What hurts? What am I carrying?*

☐ **Own**. *How is my response to my pain impacting me, my behavior,
or my relationships?*

☐ **Welcome**. *Where is God in this? What is God saying?*

_____

_____

_____

_____

_____

_____

_____

_____

_____

_____

_____

_____

_____

_____

"Solitude is not something you hope for in the future. Rather, it is a deepening of the present, and unless you look for it in the present you will never find it."
Thomas Merton

Date _____

☐ **Survey**. *Where am I?*

☐ **Lament**. *What hurts? What am I carrying?*

☐ **Own**. *How is my response to my pain impacting me, my behavior, or my relationships?*

☐ **Welcome**. *Where is God in this? What is God saying?*

_____

_____

_____

_____

_____

_____

_____

_____

_____

_____

_____

_____

_____

"Nobody, as long as he moves about among the chaotic currents of life, is without trouble."
Carl Jung

Date _____

☐ **Survey**. *Where am I?*

☐ **Lament**. *What hurts? What am I carrying?*

☐ **Own**. *How is my response to my pain impacting me, my behavior, or my relationships?*

☐ **Welcome**. *Where is God in this? What is God saying?*

_____

_____

_____

_____

_____

_____

_____

_____

_____

_____

_____

_____

"If we cannot recognize the truth, then it cannot liberate us from untruth."
James H. Cone

Date _____

☐ **Survey**. *Where am I?*

☐ **Lament**. *What hurts? What am I carrying?*

☐ **Own**. *How is my response to my pain impacting me, my behavior, or my relationships?*

☐ **Welcome**. *Where is God in this? What is God saying?*

_____

_____

_____

_____

_____

_____

_____

_____

_____

_____

_____

_____

_____

"Wisdom comes alone through suffering."
Aeschylus

Date _____

☐ **Survey**. *Where am I?*

☐ **Lament**. *What hurts? What am I carrying?*

☐ **Own**. *How is my response to my pain impacting me, my behavior, or my relationships?*

☐ **Welcome**. *Where is God in this? What is God saying?*

_____

_____

_____

_____

_____

_____

_____

_____

_____

_____

_____

_____

_____

_____

"The spiritual life is not a life before, after, or beyond our everyday experience. No, the spiritual life can only be real when it is lived in the midst of the pains and joys of the here and now."
Henri Nouwen

Date _____

☐ **Survey**. *Where am I?*

☐ **Lament**. *What hurts? What am I carrying?*

☐ **Own**. *How is my response to my pain impacting me, my behavior, or my relationships?*

☐ **Welcome**. *Where is God in this? What is God saying?*

_____

_____

_____

_____

_____

_____

_____

_____

_____

_____

_____

_____

_____

"A lack of transparency results in distrust and a deep sense of insecurity."
Dalai Lama

Date _____

☐ **Survey.** *Where am I?*

☐ **Lament.** *What hurts? What am I carrying?*

☐ **Own.** *How is my response to my pain impacting me, my behavior, or my relationships?*

☐ **Welcome.** *Where is God in this? What is God saying?*

_____

_____

_____

_____

_____

_____

_____

_____

_____

_____

_____

_____

_____

_____

*"You must let suffering speak,
if you want to hear the truth."*
Cornell West

Date _____

☐ **Survey**. *Where am I?*

☐ **Lament**. *What hurts? What am I carrying?*

☐ **Own**. *How is my response to my pain impacting me, my behavior, or my relationships?*

☐ **Welcome**. *Where is God in this? What is God saying?*

_____

_____

_____

_____

_____

_____

_____

_____

_____

_____

_____

_____

"I cannot make the universe obey me. I cannot make other people conform to my own whims and fancies. I cannot make even my own body obey me."
Thomas Merton

Date _____

☐ **Survey**. *Where am I?*

☐ **Lament**. *What hurts? What am I carrying?*

☐ **Own**. *How is my response to my pain impacting me, my behavior, or my relationships?*

☐ **Welcome**. *Where is God in this? What is God saying?*

_____

_____

_____

_____

_____

_____

_____

_____

_____

_____

_____

_____

_____

"It is a face that cannot be denied: the wickedness of others becomes our own wickedness because it kindles something evil in our own hearts."
Carl Jung

Date _____

- ☐ **Survey**. *Where am I?*

- ☐ **Lament**. *What hurts? What am I carrying?*

- ☐ **Own**. *How is my response to my pain impacting me, my behavior, or my relationships?*

- ☐ **Welcome**. *Where is God in this? What is God saying?*

_____

_____

_____

_____

_____

_____

_____

_____

_____

_____

_____

_____

_____

"I think our capacity for wholeheartedness can never be greater than our willingness to be brokenhearted. It means engaging with the world from a place of vulnerability and worthiness."
Brene Brown

Date _____

☐ **Survey**. *Where am I?*

☐ **Lament**. *What hurts? What am I carrying?*

☐ **Own**. *How is my response to my pain impacting me, my behavior, or my relationships?*

☐ **Welcome**. *Where is God in this? What is God saying?*

_____

_____

_____

_____

_____

_____

_____

_____

_____

_____

_____

_____

"Only those who have been brave enough to ride their own monsters of anger and greed, jealousy and narcissism, fear and violence all the way down to the bottom will find a truer energy with which to lead."
Ruth Haley Barton

Date _____

☐ **Survey**. *Where am I?*

☐ **Lament**. *What hurts? What am I carrying?*

☐ **Own**. *How is my response to my pain impacting me, my behavior, or my relationships?*

☐ **Welcome**. *Where is God in this? What is God saying?*

_____

_____

_____

_____

_____

_____

_____

_____

_____

_____

_____

_____

_____

"A life without a lonely place, that is, without a quiet center, becomes destructive."
Henri Nouwen

Date _____

☐ **Survey**. *Where am I?*

☐ **Lament**. *What hurts? What am I carrying?*

☐ **Own**. *How is my response to my pain impacting me, my behavior, or my relationships?*

☐ **Welcome**. *Where is God in this? What is God saying?*

_____

_____

_____

_____

_____

_____

_____

_____

_____

_____

_____

_____

_____

"The task we must set for ourselves is not to feel secure, but to be able to tolerate insecurity."
Erich Fromm

Date _____

☐ **Survey**. *Where am I?*

☐ **Lament**. *What hurts? What am I carrying?*

☐ **Own**. *How is my response to my pain impacting me, my behavior, or my relationships?*

☐ **Welcome**. *Where is God in this? What is God saying?*

_____

_____

_____

_____

_____

_____

_____

_____

_____

_____

_____

_____

_____

"When we were children, we use to think that when we were grown-up we would no longer be vulnerable. But to grow up is to accept vulnerability...To be alive is to be vulnerable."
Madeleine L'Engle

Date _____

☐ **Survey**. *Where am I?*

☐ **Lament**. *What hurts? What am I carrying?*

☐ **Own**. *How is my response to my pain impacting me, my behavior, or my relationships?*

☐ **Welcome**. *Where is God in this? What is God saying?*

_____

_____

_____

_____

_____

_____

_____

_____

_____

_____

_____

_____

_____

_____

"I imagine one of the reasons people cling to their hates so stubbornly is because they sense, once hate is gone, they will be forced to deal with pain."
James Baldwin

Date _____

☐ **Survey**. *Where am I?*

☐ **Lament**. *What hurts? What am I carrying?*

☐ **Own**. *How is my response to my pain impacting me, my behavior, or my relationships?*

☐ **Welcome**. *Where is God in this? What is God saying?*

_____

_____

_____

_____

_____

_____

_____

_____

_____

_____

_____

_____

_____

_____

"The first step toward finding God, Who is Truth, is to discover the truth about myself; and if I have been in error, this first step to truth is the discovery of my error."
Thomas Merton

Date _____

☐ **Survey**. *Where am I?*

☐ **Lament**. *What hurts? What am I carrying?*

☐ **Own**. *How is my response to my pain impacting me, my behavior, or my relationships?*

☐ **Welcome**. *Where is God in this? What is God saying?*

_____

_____

_____

_____

_____

_____

_____

_____

_____

_____

_____

_____

"Through pride we are ever deceiving ourselves. But deep down below the surface of the average conscience is a still, small voice that says to us, something is out of tune."
Carl Jung

Date _____

☐ **Survey**. *Where am I?*

☐ **Lament**. *What hurts? What am I carrying?*

☐ **Own**. *How is my response to my pain impacting me, my behavior, or my relationships?*

☐ **Welcome**. *Where is God in this? What is God saying?*

_____

_____

_____

_____

_____

_____

_____

_____

_____

_____

_____

_____

_____

"Jesus didn't say, 'Blessed are those who care for the poor.' He said, 'Blessed are we where we are poor, where we are broken.' It is there that God loves us deeply and pulls us into deeper communion."
Henri Nouwen

Date _____

☐ **Survey**. *Where am I?*

☐ **Lament**. *What hurts? What am I carrying?*

☐ **Own**. *How is my response to my pain impacting me, my behavior, or my relationships?*

☐ **Welcome**. *Where is God in this? What is God saying?*

_____

_____

_____

_____

_____

_____

_____

_____

_____

_____

_____

_____

_____

"Beware: Ignorance protects itself. Ignorance promotes suspicion. Suspicion engenders fear. Fear quails, irrational and blind, or fear looms, defiant and closed... And protected, ignorance grows."
Octavia Butler

Date _____

☐ **Survey**. *Where am I?*

☐ **Lament**. *What hurts? What am I carrying?*

☐ **Own**. *How is my response to my pain impacting me, my behavior, or my relationships?*

☐ **Welcome**. *Where is God in this? What is God saying?*

_____

_____

_____

_____

_____

_____

_____

_____

_____

_____

_____

_____

_____

"I spent a lot of years trying to outrun or outsmart vulnerability by making things certain and definite, black and white, good and bad."
Brene Brown

Date _____

☐ **Survey**. *Where am I?*

☐ **Lament**. *What hurts? What am I carrying?*

☐ **Own**. *How is my response to my pain impacting me, my behavior, or my relationships?*

☐ **Welcome**. *Where is God in this? What is God saying?*

_____

_____

_____

_____

_____

_____

_____

_____

_____

_____

_____

_____

_____

"The tighter you squeeze, the less you have."
Thomas Merton

Date _____

☐ **Survey**. *Where am I?*

☐ **Lament**. *What hurts? What am I carrying?*

☐ **Own**. *How is my response to my pain impacting me, my behavior, or my relationships?*

☐ **Welcome**. *Where is God in this? What is God saying?*

_____

_____

_____

_____

_____

_____

_____

_____

_____

_____

_____

_____

"The self is freer, because it knows itself to be finally and ultimately held safely in a Love that is unchangeable and real."
Ruth Haley Barton

Date _____

☐ **Survey.** *Where am I?*

☐ **Lament.** *What hurts? What am I carrying?*

☐ **Own.** *How is my response to my pain impacting me, my behavior, or my relationships?*

☐ **Welcome.** *Where is God in this? What is God saying?*

_____

_____

_____

_____

_____

_____

_____

_____

_____

_____

_____

_____

_____

"If there is anything that we wish to change in the child, we should first examine it and see whether it is not something that could better be changed in ourselves."
Carl Jung

Date _____

☐ **Survey**. *Where am I?*

☐ **Lament**. *What hurts? What am I carrying?*

☐ **Own**. *How is my response to my pain impacting me, my behavior, or my relationships?*

☐ **Welcome**. *Where is God in this? What is God saying?*

_____

_____

_____

_____

_____

_____

_____

_____

_____

_____

_____

_____

_____

"The most important crisis of our time is spiritual...we need places where people can grow stronger in spirit and be able to integrate the emotional struggles in their spiritual journeys."
Henri Nouwen

Date _____

☐ **Survey**. *Where am I?*

☐ **Lament**. *What hurts? What am I carrying?*

☐ **Own**. *How is my response to my pain impacting me, my behavior, or my relationships?*

☐ **Welcome**. *Where is God in this? What is God saying?*

"There can be no vulnerability without risk; there can be no community without vulnerability; there can be no peace, and ultimately no life, without community."
M. Scott Peck

Date _____

☐ **Survey**. *Where am I?*

☐ **Lament**. *What hurts? What am I carrying?*

☐ **Own**. *How is my response to my pain impacting me, my behavior, or my relationships?*

☐ **Welcome**. *Where is God in this? What is God saying?*

_____

_____

_____

_____

_____

_____

_____

_____

_____

_____

_____

_____

_____

"Nothing is more desirable than to be released from affliction, but nothing is more frightening than to be divested of a crutch."
James Baldwin

Date _____

☐ **Survey**. *Where am I?*

☐ **Lament**. *What hurts? What am I carrying?*

☐ **Own**. *How is my response to my pain impacting me, my behavior, or my relationships?*

☐ **Welcome**. *Where is God in this? What is God saying?*

_____

_____

_____

_____

_____

_____

_____

_____

_____

_____

_____

_____

_____

> *"Just remaining quietly in the presence of God, listening to him, being attentive to him, requires a lot of courage and know-how."*
> *Thomas Merton*

Date _____

☐ **Survey**. *Where am I?*

☐ **Lament**. *What hurts? What am I carrying?*

☐ **Own**. *How is my response to my pain impacting me, my behavior, or my relationships?*

☐ **Welcome**. *Where is God in this? What is God saying?*

_____

_____

_____

_____

_____

_____

_____

_____

_____

_____

_____

_____

_____

"The practice of 'turning aside to look' is a spiritual discipline that by its very nature sets us up for an encounter with God."
Ruth Haley Barton

Date _____

☐ **Survey**. *Where am I?*

☐ **Lament**. *What hurts? What am I carrying?*

☐ **Own**. *How is my response to my pain impacting me, my behavior, or my relationships?*

☐ **Welcome**. *Where is God in this? What is God saying?*

_____

_____

_____

_____

_____

_____

_____

_____

_____

_____

_____

_____

_____

"Our inclination is to show our Lord only what we feel comfortable with."
Henri Nouwen

Date _____

☐ **Survey**. *Where am I?*

☐ **Lament**. *What hurts? What am I carrying?*

☐ **Own**. *How is my response to my pain impacting me, my behavior, or my relationships?*

☐ **Welcome**. *Where is God in this? What is God saying?*

_____

_____

_____

_____

_____

_____

_____

_____

_____

_____

_____

_____

_____

_____

"My inability to lean into the discomfort of vulnerability limited the fullness of those important experiences that are wrought with uncertainty: Love, belonging, trust, joy, and creativity..."
Brene Brown

Date _____

☐ **Survey**. *Where am I?*

☐ **Lament**. *What hurts? What am I carrying?*

☐ **Own**. *How is my response to my pain impacting me, my behavior, or my relationships?*

☐ **Welcome**. *Where is God in this? What is God saying?*

_____

_____

_____

_____

_____

_____

_____

_____

_____

_____

_____

_____

*"He who learns must suffer. And even in our sleep
pain that cannot forget falls drop by drop upon the
heart, and in our own despair, against our will, comes
wisdom to us by the awful grace of God."*
Aeschylus

Date _____

☐ **Survey**. *Where am I?*

☐ **Lament**. *What hurts? What am I carrying?*

☐ **Own**. *How is my response to my pain impacting me, my behavior,
or my relationships?*

☐ **Welcome**. *Where is God in this? What is God saying?*

_____

_____

_____

_____

_____

_____

_____

_____

_____

_____

_____

_____

"The gospel of Jesus is not a rational concept to be explained in a theory of salvation, but a story about God's presence in Jesus' solidarity with the oppressed, which led to his death on the cross."
James H. Cone

Date _____

☐ **Survey**. *Where am I?*

☐ **Lament**. *What hurts? What am I carrying?*

☐ **Own**. *How is my response to my pain impacting me, my behavior, or my relationships?*

☐ **Welcome**. *Where is God in this? What is God saying?*

_____

_____

_____

_____

_____

_____

_____

_____

_____

_____

_____

_____

"We stumble and fall constantly even when we are most enlightened. But when we are in true spiritual darkness, we do not even know that we have fallen."
Thomas Merton

Date _____

☐ **Survey**. *Where am I?*

☐ **Lament**. *What hurts? What am I carrying?*

☐ **Own**. *How is my response to my pain impacting me, my behavior, or my relationships?*

☐ **Welcome**. *Where is God in this? What is God saying?*

_____

_____

_____

_____

_____

_____

_____

_____

_____

_____

_____

_____

"For a young person, it is almost a sin, or at least a danger, to be too preoccupied with himself; but for the ageing person, it is a duty and a necessity to devote serious attention to himself."
Carl Jung

Date _____

☐ **Survey**. *Where am I?*

☐ **Lament**. *What hurts? What am I carrying?*

☐ **Own**. *How is my response to my pain impacting me, my behavior, or my relationships?*

☐ **Welcome**. *Where is God in this? What is God saying?*

_____

_____

_____

_____

_____

_____

_____

_____

_____

_____

_____

_____

"The man who can articulate the movements of his inner life need no longer be victim of himself, but is able slowly and consistently to remove the obstacles that prevent the spirit from entering."
Henri Nouwen

Date _____

☐ **Survey**. *Where am I?*

☐ **Lament**. *What hurts? What am I carrying?*

☐ **Own**. *How is my response to my pain impacting me, my behavior, or my relationships?*

☐ **Welcome**. *Where is God in this? What is God saying?*

_____

_____

_____

_____

_____

_____

_____

_____

_____

_____

_____

_____

"Nobody is more dangerous than he who imagines himself pure in heart; for his purity, by definition, is unassailable."
James Baldwin

Date _____

☐ **Survey**. *Where am I?*

☐ **Lament**. *What hurts? What am I carrying?*

☐ **Own**. *How is my response to my pain impacting me, my behavior, or my relationships?*

☐ **Welcome**. *Where is God in this? What is God saying?*

_____

_____

_____

_____

_____

_____

_____

_____

_____

_____

_____

_____

_____

"A man who fears suffering is already suffering from what he fears."
Michel de Montaigne

Date _____

☐ **Survey**. *Where am I?*

☐ **Lament**. *What hurts? What am I carrying?*

☐ **Own**. *How is my response to my pain impacting me, my behavior, or my relationships?*

☐ **Welcome**. *Where is God in this? What is God saying?*

_____

_____

_____

_____

_____

_____

_____

_____

_____

_____

_____

_____

_____

"God had one son on earth without sin, but never one without suffering."
Saint Augustine

Date _____

☐ **Survey**. *Where am I?*

☐ **Lament**. *What hurts? What am I carrying?*

☐ **Own**. *How is my response to my pain impacting me, my behavior, or my relationships?*

☐ **Welcome**. *Where is God in this? What is God saying?*

_____

_____

_____

_____

_____

_____

_____

_____

_____

_____

_____

_____

*"At some point in our Christian life,
many of us realize no one ever told us how to deal
with our wounds that are still there — buried deeper
than ever — but still there."*
Ruth Haley Barton

Date _____

☐ **Survey**. *Where am I?*

☐ **Lament**. *What hurts? What am I carrying?*

☐ **Own**. *How is my response to my pain impacting me, my behavior, or my relationships?*

☐ **Welcome**. *Where is God in this? What is God saying?*

_____

_____

_____

_____

_____

_____

_____

_____

_____

_____

_____

_____

_____

"It is in this loneliness that the deepest activities begin. It is here that you discover act without motion... vision in obscurity, and, beyond all desire, a fulfillment whose limits extend to infinity."
Thomas Merton

Date _____

☐ **Survey**. *Where am I?*

☐ **Lament**. *What hurts? What am I carrying?*

☐ **Own**. *How is my response to my pain impacting me, my behavior, or my relationships?*

☐ **Welcome**. *Where is God in this? What is God saying?*

_____

_____

_____

_____

_____

_____

_____

_____

_____

_____

_____

_____

_____

"We cannot change anything until we accept it. Condemnation does not liberate, it oppresses."
Carl Jung

Date _____

☐ **Survey**. *Where am I?*

☐ **Lament**. *What hurts? What am I carrying?*

☐ **Own**. *How is my response to my pain impacting me, my behavior, or my relationships?*

☐ **Welcome**. *Where is God in this? What is God saying?*

_____

_____

_____

_____

_____

_____

_____

_____

_____

_____

_____

_____

_____

"What is redemptive is the faith that God snatches victory out of defeat, life out of death, and hope out of despair."
James H. Cone

Date _____

☐ **Survey**. *Where am I?*

☐ **Lament**. *What hurts? What am I carrying?*

☐ **Own**. *How is my response to my pain impacting me, my behavior, or my relationships?*

☐ **Welcome**. *Where is God in this? What is God saying?*

_____

_____

_____

_____

_____

_____

_____

_____

_____

_____

_____

_____

_____

_____

"The more we dare to reveal our whole trembling self to him, the more we will be able to sense that his love, which is perfect love, casts out all our fears."
Henri Nouwen

Date _____

☐ **Survey**. *Where am I?*

☐ **Lament**. *What hurts? What am I carrying?*

☐ **Own**. *How is my response to my pain impacting me, my behavior, or my relationships?*

☐ **Welcome**. *Where is God in this? What is God saying?*

_____

_____

_____

_____

_____

_____

_____

_____

_____

_____

_____

_____

"Vulnerability is the birthplace of connection and the path to the feeling of worthiness. If it doesn't feel vulnerable, the sharing is probably not constructive."
Brene Brown

Date _____

☐ **Survey**. *Where am I?*

☐ **Lament**. *What hurts? What am I carrying?*

☐ **Own**. *How is my response to my pain impacting me, my behavior, or my relationships?*

☐ **Welcome**. *Where is God in this? What is God saying?*

_____

_____

_____

_____

_____

_____

_____

_____

_____

_____

_____

_____

_____

"The individual person is responsible for living his own life and for 'finding himself.' If he persists in shifting his responsibility to somebody else, he fails to find out the meaning of his own existence."
Thomas Merton

Date _____

☐ **Survey**. *Where am I?*

☐ **Lament**. *What hurts? What am I carrying?*

☐ **Own**. *How is my response to my pain impacting me, my behavior, or my relationships?*

☐ **Welcome**. *Where is God in this? What is God saying?*

_____

_____

_____

_____

_____

_____

_____

_____

_____

_____

_____

_____

_____

_____

"Every part of the journey is of importance to the whole."
Teresa of Avila

Date _____

☐ **Survey**. *Where am I?*

☐ **Lament**. *What hurts? What am I carrying?*

☐ **Own**. *How is my response to my pain impacting me, my behavior, or my relationships?*

☐ **Welcome**. *Where is God in this? What is God saying?*

_____

_____

_____

_____

_____

_____

_____

_____

_____

_____

_____

_____

_____

_____

"Everything that irritates us about others can lead us to an understanding of ourselves."
Carl Jung

Date _____

☐ **Survey**. *Where am I?*

☐ **Lament**. *What hurts? What am I carrying?*

☐ **Own**. *How is my response to my pain impacting me, my behavior, or my relationships?*

☐ **Welcome**. *Where is God in this? What is God saying?*

_____

_____

_____

_____

_____

_____

_____

_____

_____

_____

_____

_____

"One of the most beautiful ways for spiritual formation to take place is to let your insecurity lead you closer to the Lord."
Henri Nouwen

Date _____

☐ **Survey**. *Where am I?*

☐ **Lament**. *What hurts? What am I carrying?*

☐ **Own**. *How is my response to my pain impacting me, my behavior, or my relationships?*

☐ **Welcome**. *Where is God in this? What is God saying?*

_____

_____

_____

_____

_____

_____

_____

_____

_____

_____

_____

_____

_____

"Every moment and every event of every man's life on earth plants something in his soul."
Thomas Merton

Date _____

☐ **Survey**. *Where am I?*

☐ **Lament**. *What hurts? What am I carrying?*

☐ **Own**. *How is my response to my pain impacting me, my behavior, or my relationships?*

☐ **Welcome**. *Where is God in this? What is God saying?*

_____

_____

_____

_____

_____

_____

_____

_____

_____

_____

_____

_____

_____

"Out of suffering comes the serious mind; out of salvation, the grateful heart; out of endurance, fortitude; out of deliverance, faith. Patient endurance attends to all things."
Teresa of Avila

Date _____

☐ **Survey**. *Where am I?*

☐ **Lament**. *What hurts? What am I carrying?*

☐ **Own**. *How is my response to my pain impacting me, my behavior, or my relationships?*

☐ **Welcome**. *Where is God in this? What is God saying?*

_____

_____

_____

_____

_____

_____

_____

_____

_____

_____

_____

_____

_____

"Your vision will become clear only when you can look into your own heart. Who looks outside, dreams; who looks inside, awakes."
Carl Jung

Date _____

☐ **Survey**. *Where am I?*

☐ **Lament**. *What hurts? What am I carrying?*

☐ **Own**. *How is my response to my pain impacting me, my behavior, or my relationships?*

☐ **Welcome**. *Where is God in this? What is God saying?*

_____

_____

_____

_____

_____

_____

_____

_____

_____

_____

_____

_____

_____

"We cannot embrace someone and protect ourselves from them at the same time. We have to pick one."
BrianJames McMahon

Date _____

☐ **Survey**. *Where am I?*

☐ **Lament**. *What hurts? What am I carrying?*

☐ **Own**. *How is my response to my pain impacting me, my behavior, or my relationships?*

☐ **Welcome**. *Where is God in this? What is God saying?*

_____

_____

_____

_____

_____

_____

_____

_____

_____

_____

_____

_____

_____

"The feeling remains that God is on the journey, too."
Teresa of Avila

Date _____

☐ **Survey**. *Where am I?*

☐ **Lament**. *What hurts? What am I carrying?*

☐ **Own**. *How is my response to my pain impacting me, my behavior, or my relationships?*

☐ **Welcome**. *Where is God in this? What is God saying?*

_____

_____

_____

_____

_____

_____

_____

_____

_____

_____

_____

_____

_____

_____

"Knowing your own darkness is the best method for dealing with the darkness of other people."
Carl Jung

Date _____

- ☐ **Survey**. *Where am I?*

- ☐ **Lament**. *What hurts? What am I carrying?*

- ☐ **Own**. *How is my response to my pain impacting me, my behavior, or my relationships?*

- ☐ **Welcome**. *Where is God in this? What is God saying?*

_____

_____

_____

_____

_____

_____

_____

_____

_____

_____

_____

_____

_____

"Our human compassion binds us the one to the other – not in pity or patronizingly, but as human beings who have learnt how to turn our common suffering into hope for the future."
Nelson Mandela

Date _____

- ☐ **Survey**. *Where am I?*

- ☐ **Lament**. *What hurts? What am I carrying?*

- ☐ **Own**. *How is my response to my pain impacting me, my behavior, or my relationships?*

- ☐ **Welcome**. *Where is God in this? What is God saying?*

_____

_____

_____

_____

_____

_____

_____

_____

_____

_____

_____

_____

_____

"We are most often lost, not because we do not know where we are going, but because we do not know where we are."
BrianJames McMahon

Date _____

☐ **Survey**. *Where am I?*

☐ **Lament**. *What hurts? What am I carrying?*

☐ **Own**. *How is my response to my pain impacting me, my behavior, or my relationships?*

☐ **Welcome**. *Where is God in this? What is God saying?*

_____

_____

_____

_____

_____

_____

_____

_____

_____

_____

_____

_____

_____

_____

"In the inner stillness where meditation leads, the Spirit secretly anoints the soul and heals our deepest wounds."
John of the Cross

Date _____

☐ **Survey**. *Where am I?*

☐ **Lament**. *What hurts? What am I carrying?*

☐ **Own**. *How is my response to my pain impacting me, my behavior, or my relationships?*

☐ **Welcome**. *Where is God in this? What is God saying?*

_____

_____

_____

_____

_____

_____

_____

_____

_____

_____

_____

_____

_____

"For everyone who exalts himself will be humbled, and everyone who humbles himself will be exalted."
Jesus Christ

Date _____

☐ **Survey**. *Where am I?*

☐ **Lament**. *What hurts? What am I carrying?*

☐ **Own**. *How is my response to my pain impacting me, my behavior, or my relationships?*

☐ **Welcome**. *Where is God in this? What is God saying?*

_____

_____

_____

_____

_____

_____

_____

_____

_____

_____

_____

_____

_____

"There is no easy walk to freedom anywhere, and many of us will have to pass through the valley of the shadow of death again and again before we reach the mountaintop of our desires."
Nelson Mandela

Date _____

☐ **Survey**. *Where am I?*

☐ **Lament**. *What hurts? What am I carrying?*

☐ **Own**. *How is my response to my pain impacting me, my behavior, or my relationships?*

☐ **Welcome**. *Where is God in this? What is God saying?*

_____

_____

_____

_____

_____

_____

_____

_____

_____

_____

_____

_____

_____

"Oh, how everything that is suffered with love is healed again!"
Teresa of Avila

Date _____

☐ **Survey**. *Where am I?*

☐ **Lament**. *What hurts? What am I carrying?*

☐ **Own**. *How is my response to my pain impacting me, my behavior, or my relationships?*

☐ **Welcome**. *Where is God in this? What is God saying?*

_____

_____

_____

_____

_____

_____

_____

_____

_____

_____

_____

_____

_____

Journal

a guide toward groundedness

ABOUT THE CREATOR

BrianJames McMahon is a licensed marriage and family therapist, consultant, and business coach. He lives in Kansas City, where he co-directs a group counseling practice that trains, equips, and launches therapists into private practice who are clinically sound, professionally competent, and personally growing. As a therapist he works with pastors, therapists, and entrepreneurs to find healing from pain, overcome barriers to connection, unlock potential, and grow into who they are becoming. Learn more about his work as a therapist at www.brianjamestherapy.com. BrianJames works as a consultant with churches, community organizations, and businesses to develop cultures and environments that are emotional and relational safe for their people. Learn more about his work as a consultant at www.brianjamesconsulting.com.

WHY THE SLOW JOURNAL WAS CREATED

The SLOW journal exists because you matter. You were designed by God, are seen by God, and are invited by God to continue to grow into who you are becoming.

I spent years in personal reflection and working with others to find ways to slow down, regain our footing in a fast-paced world, and reclaim attentiveness to where we are, who we are, and where we are going. This journal is a guide toward that. Toward slowing down. Toward finding ways to get our feet on the ground in a balanced, whole-self manner that returns us to attentiveness to God and to the invitation that God has for us. In the same way that a sailboat adrift in a lake that has lost its steering is guided by a tugboat back to shore, so this journal has been created to help guide you back to your mooring, to a place your feet can feel stable on the floor beneath them, and your soul can feel grounded.

Thank you for your courage to engage these practices.
May you continue to experience healing as you grow into
who you are becoming.

Order your SLOW Journal below: